QUILTING 201

Beyond the Basics

How to measure, cut, and make triangle squares, flying geese and more; how to include sashing, borders and miter corners; layout design alternatives

by
Sharon Hultgren

Second Book in the
Learning to Quilt The Easy Way
Book and Video Series

EZ INTERNATIONAL
95 Mayhill Street
Saddle Brook, NJ 07662

Photography by Michael Keefe, St. Paul, Minnesota.

Graphics and layout by SPPS, Inc, Las Vegas, Nevada.

Published in the United States by EZ International, 95 Mayhill Street, Saddle Brook, NJ 07662.
Printed in Hong Kong.   99 98 97 96 95 94
                          9 8 7 6 5 4 3 2

ISBN: 1-881588-06-8

Welcome to the second book of the Learning to Quilt The Easy Way series. In this book we will work with triangles, color placement, secondary blocks, and more. The tools used will be the Easy Angle™, Easy Angle II™, Companion Angle™, the Quickline© Ruler and the Super Quickline© ruler. As you work with the designs in this book it is my hope that they become the springboard for designs of your own.

Table of Contents

Projects

Getting Started

Defining a Quilt. A quilt consists basically of three layers: the top, the back and a layer of batting sandwiched between. The three layers are sewn or tied together.

There are numerous types of *quilt tops*. Most can be included in the following list.

- The top layer can be a solid piece of fabric where the quilting rather than the piecing creates the beauty of the finished product. This is called a white on white or shole cloth quilt.

- The top layer can also be what is referred to as an *appliqué quilt* in which solid pieces of fabric shapes are appliquéd to the top.

- *Pieced quilts* consist of geometric shapes that are sewn together to form a design. These can be made very simply or with thousands of small pieces sewn in a detailed design. In the *Quilt The Easy Way* series of booklets, we primarily work with pieced quilts.

- The *crazy quilt* is made of irregular shapes that overlap and have decorative stitching around each piece.

- Of course, there are combinations of these (e.g., a pieced top with large, plain, light colored blocks for fancy quilting, alternated with pieced blocks.)

The main approach to construction for the projects in this series of booklets is *strip piecing*. As opposed to cutting pieces using templates, strips of fabric will be cut the proper width, and pieces will be cut from the strips using simple measurements and accurate tools.

The center layer of a quilt is called *batting*. It can be very thin or very thick and is made from cotton, wool, silk or polyester.

The bottom layer is the *backing*. This can be a solid piece of fabric or pieces sewn together. A separate design might be used here.

Choosing and Preparing the Fabric. A quilt should be made from 100% cotton fabrics because it is easy to sew and easy to care for. Cotton/Polyester blends have a tendency to stretch while sewing and to "pill" when used.

A **quilt** consists of three layers – the top, the batting, and the backing – sewn or tied together.

Piecing is the construction of the quilt.

Quilting is the process of stitching the three layers together.

Strip Piecing is the process of cutting strips of fabric and then cutting pieces from strips. This method uses measurements and tools versus cutting pieces using templates.

A **"tone on tone"** fabric is one that appears to be a solid color but has a patter n that is a deeper tone of the same color.

Tools for strip cutting: **Rotary Cutter, Mat, Acrylic Rulers**.

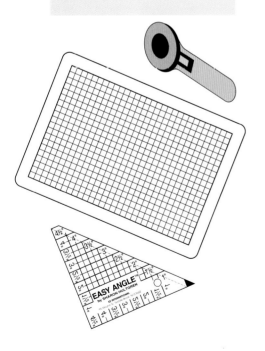

To prepare the fabric for sewing, some teachers will tell you to prewash the fabric and others will say not to prewash. I prefer to prewash (using a mild soap that does not have bleach in it) to prevent shrinkage, dyes bleeding, and to eliminate the chemical finishes that are found on most fabrics. After the fabric has been prewashed it must be pressed to remove wrinkles.

When I want the completed quilt to have an "old-fashioned" look, I make an exception to prewashing. However, I do test the fabrics that will be used in the quilt for color fastness and color bleeding. A quick and simple way is to soak a snip from each fabric to be used in the quilt in a sink of warm water. If no color runs, I go one step further and rub each piece of fabric together with another. If no color rubs off on another piece, I use them with confidence. If any color rubs off of a piece of fabric, I do not use it.

Choosing color for many new quilters is the most difficult task. There is such a wonderful array of color available to quilters today, it is hard to know where to start. Work with colors you enjoy and explore colors with the varied designs in this booklet.

If three fabrics are needed, a print, a solid, and a "tone on tone" fabric would be a good range to work with. A "tone on tone" fabric is one that appears to be a solid color but has a pattern that is a deeper tone of the same color.

For any quilt you make, watch for a nice blend in the colors and notice if one color "jumps" out at you. This may be good or bad, depending on the pattern you are making. For example, if you are making a star quilt, you want the stars to "pop" away from the background. Therefore, the stars must be made of the strongest colors.

Before cutting and sewing the entire quilt, it is a good idea to cut and make one or two blocks first. This will give you the opportunity to change the color positions in the blocks, or the change the fabrics before you make a quilt you won't like.

The *tools* you need to make the projects in this quilting series are most important. A *rotary cutter* is important for smooth, fast cutting through more than one or more layers of fabric. Remember to keep a sharp blade in your rotary cutter. The cutter must be used on a special mat that will not be cut apart by the sharp blade. A *cutting mat* that has 1" grid markings and is at least 24"x 34" is a good one. Most mats are sensitive to heat and will warp when left in the sun or near a hot surface, so be careful. Finally, a good *thick acrylic ruler* is a must for use as a guide in cutting. EZ International Quickline Ruler™, Super Quickline Ruler™, Easy Angle™, Easy Angle II™, Easy Eight™, Easy Six™, Easy Hexagon™, Easy Three™, and Companion Angle™ are thick acrylic rulers used in the projects in this series. Tools used in the projects of a specific booklet are discussed in that booklet.

Other tools required for quilt making are a sewing machine that is cleaned and oiled and able to sew a nice straight stitch, fabric scissors, pins, good thread, and a seam ripper.

Where you sew is important for the enjoyment of piecing and quilting. It is best to have an area that can be left "as is" – not a good idea for the dining room table! An ironing board lowered to table height and positioned to the left of your sewing machine will encourage you to press often, which is important. A good iron that can be used with or without steam and a secretarial chair that gives you good back support are also nice to have. Good lighting is a must – a window on your left will give good light and inspiration, but a swing arm office lamp providing light from the left will substitute. A cutting table that is counter height (the kitchen counter is great) saves your back! You can tack a design board to a wall so you can build your quilt and study your design process. The board can be made of rigid styrofoam (purchased from a lumber yard) and covered with felt or flannel.

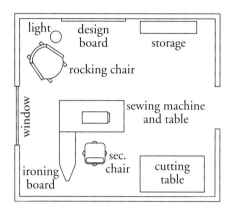

It is often told that when children leave home they return to find "their room" is now Mom's quilting room! This is all very nice, but not necessary. Some wonderful quilts have been made on a card table in the corner of the dining room!

Cutting and Piecing Tips

Straightening Fabric and Cutting Strips. Use a gridded cutting mat for fabric and tool alignment. When I cut, I use the Quickline® ruler. Refer to page 11 for instructions in its general use.

First, fold your fabric pieces in half, matching the selvage edges. Lay the fabric on your gridded cutting mat. Line up the selvage and fold edges as close as possible to the vertical grid lines of the mat. If the raw edges are not square, first square up the edges. To do this, match the lines on the Quickline® ruler with those on the cutting mat from side to side, placing the ruler over the bottom edge of the fabric. The excess fabric should always be in front of you and above the ruler. Trim along the top edge of the ruler. Discard the trimmed edge.

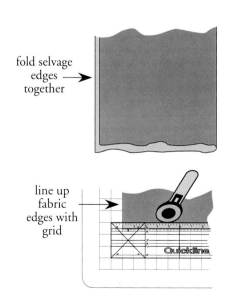

fold selvage edges together

line up fabric edges with grid

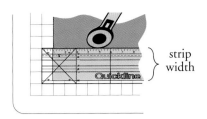

strip width

To cut strips, you will use the same mat grid alignment technique. Align the fabric edges with the mat. Then place the ruler on the fabric with the appropriate line on the ruler over the bottom edge of the fabric. The distance from the top of the ruler to the bottom of the fabric should be the desired strip width to cut. With the rotary cutter, cut along the top edge of the ruler.

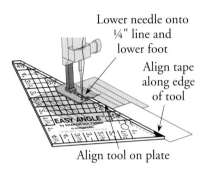

Lower needle onto ¼" line and lower foot

Align tape along edge of tool

Align tool on plate

Sewing a ¼" seam allowance is a very important step for accurate machine work. I find that it is good to leave the needle in the center position. To mark your machine with ¼" seam allowance, take a ruler or tool (e.g., Easy Angle™) that has a good quarter inch marking on it and gently set the sewing machine needle down on the ruler on the ¼" line. Place a piece of masking tape on the machine right next to the ruler, but do not cover the feed dogs. This will be your ¼" mark for all of your quiltmaking seams. All the tools and patterns in this series are designed using a ¼" seam.

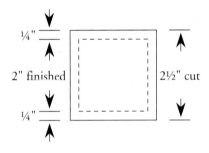

¼"

2" finished

2½" cut

¼"

When measuring to determine cut sizes, you will always add ¼" to each edge of a finished piece. For example, if squares are to be cut and the finished size of the square is 2" x 2", you will cut strips 2½" and cut squares from them 2½" x 2½"

Some tools used in subsequent booklets automatically incorporate seam allowances. These tools are the Easy Eight™, Easy Six™, Easy Three™, and Easy Hexagon™.

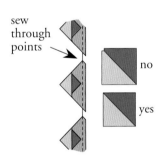

sew through points

no

yes

Chain Sewing. Once you are satisfied with your choice of fabrics, and have started a project, you will be sewing several of the same units at one time. Chain sewing helps the project step along more quickly, since you don't have to lift the needle and take these pieces away from the sewing machine until you are done sewing them all. After sewing them, you can take them away from the machine and snip them apart. They will then be ready for pressing. However, when sewing triangle pairs, make sure you sew through the "point" to avoid leaving a little "box" in one corner of the resulting square.

Pinning. To keep seams in place when sewing larger units together, pin at the seam intersections.

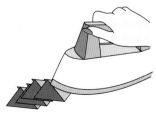

Pressing. I think it is necessary to press often during the course of a project. This helps to keep seams straight and the widths of the units you are piecing accurate. When you are pressing pieces you have chain sewn, use stack pressing. When you stack press, you will simply press pieces over the top of previously pressed pieces. For the most part press seams to one side rather than open. I try to press units so that, when they are placed right sides together with other units for sewing, seams will not overlap, but will lay in opposite directions. They sort of "snuggle" together. This helps keep the seam intersections accurate and easier to sew.

Finishing the Quilt

Borders. Borders can be an important part of a quilt. Some say that a quilt without a border is like a picture without a frame. Even though we often see older quilts without them, borders do give a finished look to the edge of a quilt. Some more elaborate borders become an important part of the quilt design. The fabrics in the border should also be used in the quilt top.

Simple Borders. After completing piecing of your quilt top, you may add simple borders.

If you are sure of piecing accuracy, you can add the dimensions of the pieces to get the total dimension. For example, if there are four 8" blocks, the unfinished dimension would be 32" + ½" (two seam allowances). When you measure, first measure the top and bottom of the quilt top. If measurements are different, use the smaller number. It is better to ease in a little excess than to stretch the side. Cut two strips this length, with a strip width equal to the finished width you want plus two seam allowances. Attach the borders on the top and bottom of the quilt top.

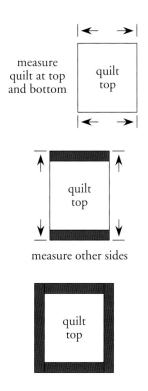

Next, measure or calculate the length of the quilt top with the border attached to the top and bottom. Cut strips this length using the required strip width. Attach these strips to the sides. If borders are longer than your strips, sew strips together end-to-end to get additional length. Use the same method to add additional borders if you wish. Once borders are attached, you are ready to complete the quilt.

Mitered Borders. These corners are not difficult but do take more fabric. The border strip must be as long as the side of the unfinished quilt top to which it will be attached plus two times the unfinished border strip width.

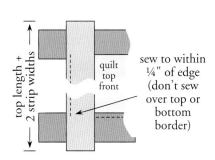

Center each strip on the appropriate side and sew to within ¼" of each quilt top corner. *Be careful not to sew on the adjacent border strips.*

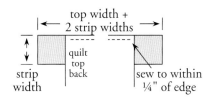

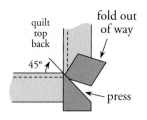

At each corner, turn one strip back out of the way and fold the other one at a 45° angle. You can check the angle using Easy Angle™ or Easy Angle II™. Press it to make a crease, without stretching.

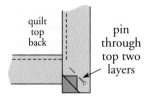

Next, fold the other strip up over the creased strip, and pin the two ends together. *Put the pin through the first two layers only.* Then fold the quilt top at the 45° angle so the two border strips lay over one another. Stitch on the crease.

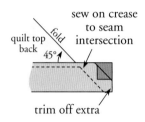

Trim the excess to within ¼" of the stitch line. Unfold the quilt top and press the seam open.

Multiple Borders and Corner Treatments. Although border width varies between borders, all sides of a border should probably be of equal width. Multiple smaller borders are better than a single wide one, unless you want an elaborate quilt design in it. Remember that quilting shows up best on light, solid colors. There should not be more than 4 borders on the side of a full size quilt. The width should not exceed 14" per side.

The first type is the simple box or stair step border. As in the simple border, additional borders are added to the top and bottom first, then to the sides. Measuring for length is the same.

Placing fabric squares or blocks in the corners can give a decorative look. Fabric squares can be helpful if you are running out of fabric, and can be a place for fancy quilting.

When you want to miter a border that has several fabrics in it, you can sew the strips together first and then miter them all at once. However, there is considerable waste, and you might consider mitering each border separately.

There are three options for completing the quilt (leaving it in a bottom drawer or a trunk is not one of them!):

- Turn and tie
- Baste and machine quilt.
- Baste and hand quilt.

The first option does not use a binding, and is discussed in detail in the first quilt design, *Four by Four*, in the first booklet of this series, *The Basics*. The discussion below addresses the last two approaches.

Marking the quilt. For design quilting it is easiest to mark the quilt before basting the batting and backing on. Before marking your quilt top, test the marking utensil you are using to make sure the marks will come off. A soft lead pencil, chalk pencil or one that is marketed as a quilting pencil should always work. It is still best to test whatever you decide to use. There are plastic stencils with quilting designs in them. You simply guide your pencil in the laser cut lines. It is very nice to mix these designs with a background fill pattern. Fill patterns can be straight lines as close as ½" -1" apart that make diamonds or squares or they can be tiny little stitches that seem to have no pattern at all. In traditional quilts the more stitching the better! The same process of marking can be used for quilts that are going to be machine quilted.

Basting the quilt. The backing should be washed and pressed unless you have planned for the "old look". It's okay for the backing to have a seam in it. The backing should be at least 3" larger than the quilt top all the way around.

The batting should be taken out of the package the night before it is to be used. This gives it a chance to relax so the creases and folds will not be a problem. It is possible to fluff it in the clothes dryer as well. If you are using a natural fiber batt (e.g., wool) follow the package directions.

Before basting, stabilize the backing. This can be done by taping it wrong side up to a large table, or by pinning it to the carpet with large "T" pins. Next, gently lay the batting on top of the backing. Use a yardstick to smooth out any wrinkles. Then lay the pieced top on the batting, right side up. It is very important that the quilt be "square". Now with a large needle and a long piece of quilting thread, make large stitches in rows about 6" apart. Begin in the center, if possible, or at one end. When the entire quilt is basted you will be able to lift the quilt and work with it. Another basting technique, which is especially good for machine quilting, is to use 1" safety pins every 5 to 6 inches. Pin from the center out. Now you are ready to quilt.

Quilting. To hand quilt you should use quilting thread and a #8, 9, 10, or 12 quilting needle. These needles will seem small to you but it is important in being able to use a thimble. The #8 is larger than the #12. The quilting stitch is simply a running stitch made with small even stitches that go through the three layers with each stitch. To begin quilting set a knot in the end of a 24" length of thread. Set the needle into the quilt ¾" away from where the actual stitching is to begin. Run the needle in the layer batting and come up into the quilt top where you want to begin stitching. Pull the

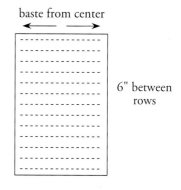

baste from center

6" between rows

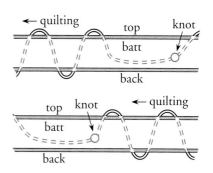

thread and "pop" the knot into the batting layer. Take small, even stitches. When the thread becomes too short to use, make a knot on top of the quilt, set the needle in next to the knot and run the needle in the batting for about ¾", bring the needle up and pull the thread to set the knot into the quilt.

There are many designs that are possible for each quilt. One method is called "stitching in the ditch". This is a line of stitching right next to the seam line. If the seam allowances are pressed to the left then the quilting is to be done on the right side of the seam. This quilting is hardly seen but it does secure the layers. Another form is ¼" away from the seam on either side of the seam. This is often considered the most traditional but very time consuming. For a perfect quarter inch distance the line is either marked or ¼" masking tape is used.

A new and exciting machine quilting aid, Stitch Thru™ eliminates the marking process. After the quilt is basted you simply put a special paper that has quilting lines marked on it onto your quilt and sew on the stitching lines. When you are finished sewing the paper gently tears away!

There are several fine books available on machine quilting. Basically if your sewing machine can "darn" it will quilt! Drop or cover the feed dogs, use a darning foot and you will be able to do free motion quilting. A walking foot is necessary for straight line machine quilting. With machine quilting being so widely accepted I believe we will be the generation of quilt finishers! There will not be trunks of quilt tops left for the next generation!

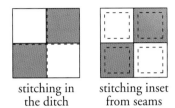

stitching in   stitching inset
the ditch   from seams

Sample
Stitch-Thru™
Designs

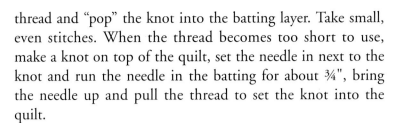

stitch through paper
and tear away

Binding. The binding finishes the edge of your quilt. It should be made of one of the materials used somewhere else in the quilt. I like to cut 2½" strips of fabric for my binding. I do not cut bias binding unless it is for a curved edge. It is a good idea to cut the binding strips when you are sewing the quilt so that you will be sure to have the same fabric available when it is time to sew the binding on. This could be six months from when you started the project!

First, cut strips of your binding fabric the required width (e.g., 2½"). If you need additional length, sew strips together end-to-end. Fold the corner of the strip down as shown. Then fold the left edge to meet the right edge.

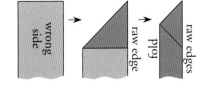

wrong side   fold   raw edge   raw edges

Set the binding ¼" from the edge of the border of the quilt. The initial placement should be somewhere away from the corner, because the end that you folded will have to join with the opposite end of another piece, shown below. Pin the binding. Be careful not to stretch the edge of the quilt, since you want to keep the borders on the opposite sides equal. Stitch ½" from the edge of the binding.

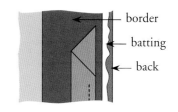

When you come to the corner stop ½" from the end of the quilt border. Take the needle out of the quilt and cut the thread leaving 3" of thread. Turn the quilt to begin working on the next side. Fold the binding up as shown, and then down, with the fold being even with the edge of the border. Begin stitching ½" from the edge of the border.

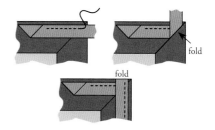

After completing all four sides tuck the end of the binding into the fold made at the beginning to complete the binding. You will have a nicely finished edge where the binding strips meet. Sew over this join as indicated.

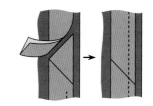

Finally, turn the binding to the back. Fold the corners back and make a mitered corner and stitch. Use a blind stitch to sew the binding to the back of the quilt.

Signing and dating your quilt. It is very important that you sign and date the quilt you have just finished. If it is your very first quilt, you will want to remember when you started your quilting journey. If it is a gift, it is important that in the future, people will know where and by whom the quilt was made.

Tool Tutorial

The tools used for the projects in this booklet are the Quickline® and Super Quickline® Rulers, Easy Angle™, and Easy Angle II™, and Companion Angle™ These tools are accurately marked and are made of heavy acrylic, making it easy to accurately cut fabric with a rotary cutter. The following discussions show the main uses of the tools for the projects in this booklet. Each booklet in the *Quilt the Easy Way* series addresses tools specific to the projects it presents.

You may find further specialized uses of tools as you become more familiar with them.

Quickline® and Super Quickline® Rulers

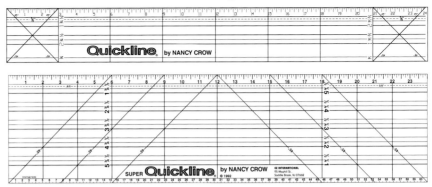

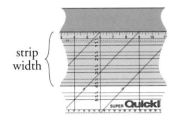

strip width

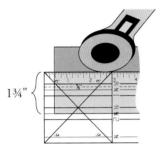

1¾"

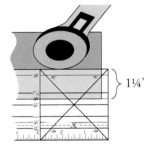

1¼"

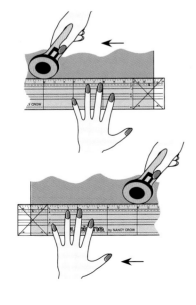

These rulers are very handy for straightening the bottom edge of your fabric (see page 5) and for accurately cutting strips. The Quickline® ruler is 3" wide for cutting narrower strips, and the Super Quickline Ruler® is 6" wide for cutting wider strips. Both rulers are accurately marked with lines along the length of the ruler that allow you to measure width in ¼" increments. These lines indicate the distance from the edge of the ruler. Both rulers are 24" long which allows for cutting single folded (selvage to selvage) fabric.

Cut strips by lining the base of the straightened fabric along the line indicating the width of the strip to be cut, and, while holding the ruler steady, cutting along the edge of the ruler with a rotary cutter.

Although there are not lines every ¼" on the rulers, you may measure any ¼" increment from at least one of the long edges. For example, you can measure 1¾" from the top, but there is no line to measure 1¼" from the top. However, you can turn the ruler around so the bottom is at the top, and then measure down 1¼".

Remember, when determining the width of the strip to cut, add two seam allowances to the desired *finished* width. The seam allowance used in all projects in this series is an accurate ¼".

You may find it best when cutting to cut across the body. Place the ruler so that you cut from your right to your left. If you are left handed, cut from your left to your right. With one hand hold the ruler down below where you cut. Cut part of the way across, stop cutting, lift the hand holding the ruler, and move the hand over to hold down the other end, then continue cutting. This reduces the chance of the ruler slipping as you cut.

Easy Angle™ and Easy Angle II™

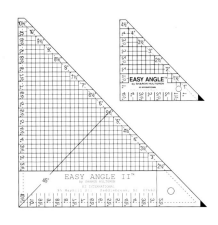

Easy Angle™ and Easy Angle II™ provide a quick method to cut right triangles for half square triangles or triangle squares. Just add seam allowance to your finished size and cut strips this width. Place two cut strips of fabric right sides together, then cut with the Easy Angle™ or Easy Angle II™. The lines on the tool are provided at ¼" increments, and are used for aligning fabric strips for cutting. The heavier lines are provided at ½" increments. Easy Angle™ yields unfinished triangles of 1" to 4½". Easy Angle II™ yields unfinished triangles of 2½" to 10½". The discussion below is for Easy Angle™, but it equally applies to Easy Angle II™.

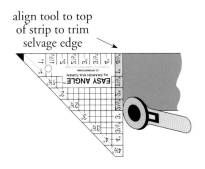

align tool to top of strip to trim selvage edge

Use of the tool requires that you select a finished square size. Once you do this, add ½" to get the corresponding unfinished triangle size. Cut strips the unfinished width of the triangle size. Lay the strips right sides together. For each strip or pair of strips, align the bottom of the tool over the top of the strip(s) as shown, and trim the selvage edge.

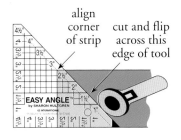

align corner of strip   cut and flip across this edge of tool

Align the bottom of the tool on the bottom edge of the strip. Slide the tool to the right until the end of the strip aligns with the strip width number along the diagonal edge. The entire number must be on the fabric (as shown). Cut along the diagonal edge of the tool.

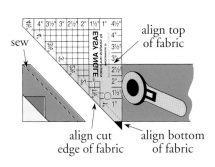

sew   align top of fabric

align cut edge of fabric   align bottom of fabric

Flip the tool over the long edge and align the tool so that the cut edge of the fabric aligns with the strip width number and the bottom edge of the fabric aligns with the top of the black triangle on the tool. Cut along the perpendicular edge of the tool.

Repeat these last two steps until you have cut all of your triangles. You will have pairs of triangles which you may chain sew (see page 8) to make the triangle-squares. Note that the triangles are already right sides together. Simply sew, open up and press seam to one side.

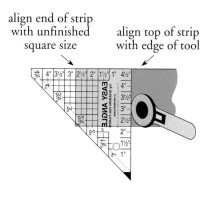

align end of strip with unfinished square size

align top of strip with edge of tool

To make single fabric squares up to 4½" using Easy Angle™ (or up to 10½" using Easy Angle II™), cut a strip equal to the unfinished square size. Align the tool with the top edge of the strip and slide it along the strip until the left side of the strip aligns with the vertical line on the tool representing the unfinished square size. The entire number must be on the fabric.

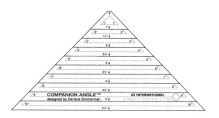

Companion Angle™

Use Companion Angle™ to cut triangles with the long edge on the outside of a block, border, or quilt. Cut the triangles with the long edge on the straight of the grain to prevent distortion.

Dashed lines represent sewing lines and show the *finished* triangle size, based on a ¼" seam allowance; center numbers represent the width of the strip to cut; solid lines underneath are used for alignment (for example, cut a 2½" strip for *finished* 4" triangles.)

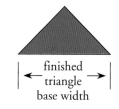

finished triangle base width

Determine the required size of the long edge of your finished triangle.

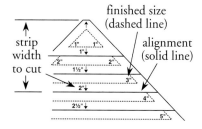

finished size (dashed line)

strip width to cut

alignment (solid line)

Determine the required strip width to cut to get the desired triangle size. This will be the distance from the top of the tool to the solid line immediately below the dashed line corresponding to the triangle finished base width.

Cut strips as required. Lay the tool on top of the strip so you can read the tool name. Then align the top of the tool with the top of the strip, the appropriate solid line with the bottom of the strip. Cut on both sides to get one triangle.

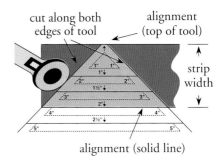

Turn the tool upside down and align the side of the tool with the end of the strip, the top of the tool with the bottom of the strip, and the top of the strip with the appropriate solid line. Cut on the right side of the tool to get the next triangle. Next, turn the tool right side up again, align and cut on the right side. Continue with these steps until you have the necessary triangles.

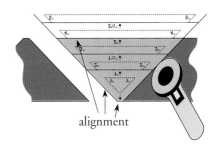

To get trapezoids, first determine the finished base or top length size and the finished height. Add ½" to the finished height. Cut strips this width.

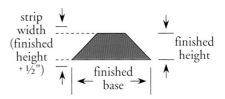

Find the dashed line on the tool labeled with the finished base or top length, and the associated solid line beneath the dashed line. Align this solid line on the bottom or top of the strip. Cut the first trapezoid by cutting on both sides. Turn the tool upside down. Line up the end of the strip with the left side of the tool and the top of the strip with the appropriate solid line. Cut along the right side of the tool. Turn the tool right side up and continue in this manner.

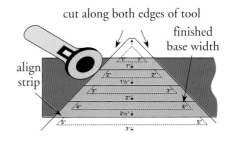

Shoo-Fly

Shoo-Fly		
Size	Across	43" x 51"
	Down	4 blocks
		5 blocks
		plus sashing
Fabric (yd)	Green	1½
	Floral	¾
	Cream	1
	Accent	¼
Strips to Cut	Green	11 - 2½"
		5 - 4"
	Floral	3 - 6½"
	Cream	6 - 2½"
	Accent	5 - 1½"
Blocks		20
		49
		30

The Shoo-Fly block is a nine-patch block that looks good when placed in a sashed setting. You can make this block with two primary fabrics, a light (cream) and a dark (green). Add a medium fabric for the the sashing (a floral looks nice) and use the dark fabric to set between sashing strips at the block corners and you have a beautiful quilt. You can add borders to frame the blocks and sashing. I have included an accent strip for the inside border, and the dark fabric as the outside border.

The fabric I used for the accent strip was of a bright color that appears in the floral print I used for the sashing strips.

The directions for this quilt use a 6" finished block with 2" finished sashing. Therefore, since the block is a nine-patch, the pieces in the blocks and sashing are cut from 2½" strips.

Begin by measuring and cutting the required number of strips of each fabric. Before making all the blocks, cut pieces for and make a single block using the provided directions. In this way, you can be sure of the colors you are using before making all of the blocks in the quilt.

To make the blocks, cut the triangles and squares from the strips of green and cream fabric. Remember to make one block first before cutting pieces for all blocks.

Place green 2½" strips on cream 2½" strips right sides together, with the cream strip on top. Cut 4 triangles for each block using the Easy Angle™. You will cut a total of 80 of these pairs of triangles.

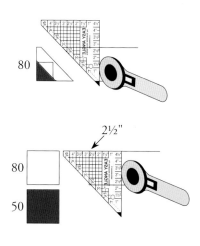

From the remaining green and cream strips, cut four 2½" cream squares and one 2½" green square for each block. Cut an additional 30 squares from the green fabric for use in the sashing. You will need a total 80 cream squares and 50 green squares.

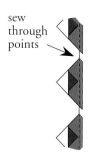

Without opening up the pairs of triangles, chain-sew them together as defined in the *Cutting and Piecing Tips* section, starting on page 5. Make sure you sew each pair together starting at the "point" and maintain the ¼" seam. Continue to sew each of the triangle pairs without lifting the needle.

Now clip the triangle squares apart and press the seam allowance toward the green fabric. It is best to press with a hot dry iron. This will not distort the fabric or burn your fingers. Also, press on the top or right side of the fabric. By doing this a pleat will not develop next to the seam. Employ stack pressing as defined in *Cutting and Piecing Tips*.

Set the blocks out in the manner they will be finished. Sew the squares together in rows as shown. Sew the left squares and center squares right sides together, then add the right squares.

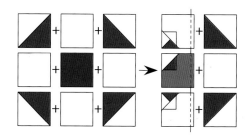

Clip the rows apart and press the seam allowances toward the darker fabric. Sew the center row to one of the others right sides together. Open up and press the seam toward the center row. Place the third row right sides together with the row to which it is to be sewn (top or bottom). Sew, open up, and press the seam toward the center.

The blocks are now complete. The outside edges should be even, the seam intersections should match and there should be ¼" between the edge of the block and the point of the triangle. The block should measure 6½". How did you do? Make a total of 20 blocks in this manner.

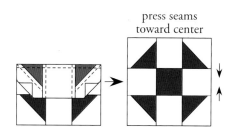

press seams toward center

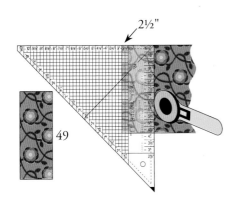

2½"

49

Now cut the remaining pieces for the sashing. You have already cut the dark green squares. With the Easy Angle II™ cross-cut 49 - 2½" wide strips from the 6½" strips of the floral fabric.

Lay out the pieces in rows of sashing strips and green squares alternated with rows of sashing strips and Shoo-Fly blocks. The sashing rows will have 5 green squares alternated with four sashing strips. The block rows will have 5 sashing strips alternated with 4 Shoo-Fly blocks.

press seams

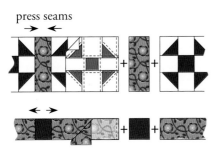

Complete the block rows first. Sew the sashing strips to the sides of the blocks. Be very careful to match the top and bottom edges. Press the seam allowances toward the sashing strips.

Next sew the sashing strips and green squares together, with the sashing strips lengthwise. Press the seam allowances toward the sashing strips.

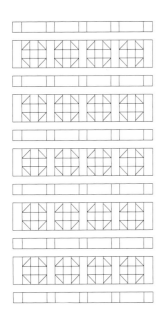

Finally, sew the rows together from the top to the bottom. You may want to pin the seams together before sewing to make sure that they don't move while you sew and they line up when you are done. Be careful to remove the pins as you sew.

Note that if the sashing squares were not used in rows, it would have been necessary to mark the sashing strips between the block rows to ensure that the corresponding blocks in each row were aligned vertically.

The first border is an accent border using the 1½" accent strips. Much like the matting on a framed picture. Sew the strips across the top and bottom first. The side borders will have to be pieced. Do not add a small piece on the very end. It looks much better to have at least 12 inches before a seam is used. So begin stitching with the small piece that has been added on. The outside border is added in the same way using remaining 2½" green strips. If a strip is too short, simply add another strip by sewing them together end-to-end.

Refer to the *Finishing the Quilt* section, starting on page 6, when adding the batting and backing, quilting and binding. You will need 1½ yards of fabric for the backing. Place backing right side down, with batting on top of it, followed by the quilt top right side up. Fix these to a flat surface and pin or baste.

Quilt as desired and add the binding.

Design & Layout Options

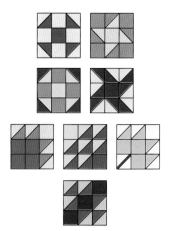

There are a myriad of different nine-patch (3 x 3) blocks, based on placement of squares and triangles and color. However, there are some general categories into which we can place them based on how we can use them in a quilt layout. These categories are listed below.

- Blocks that look the same no matter how you rotate them

- Blocks that can be turned four ways

- Blocks that can be turned two ways only

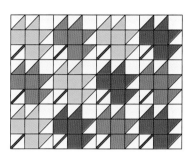

Varying the color between blocks in a design gives you many more layout options. Design 1 shows all blocks in the same orientation, but with a variety of colors.

Design 2 shows one layout for a block that can be turned four ways. Note in the upper left corner we have placed four of the blocks in the four possible orientations, and we have repeated this set of four. Doesn't this look nice? Rearranging the four blocks will give a completely different look.

Design 3 shows what happens when we alternate the two possible turns of one block that only has two turning options. Can you picture it with all blocks turned the same way?

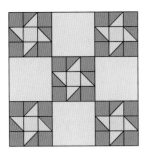

Design 4 includes secondary blocks. This breaks up the design for blocks which look the same no matter how they are turned. You must have an uneven number of rows for this design so primary blocks appear in each corner.

In design 5 the primary and secondary blocks are set on point and corner and side triangles are added. In addition, corner triangles have been added to the secondary blocks.

Design 6 includes sashing strips, another option for breaking up a design. Here we have sashing squares interspersed with sashing strips, which gives more design options, and helps in aligning blocks.

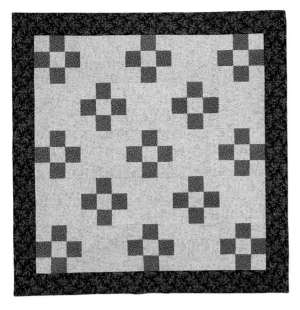

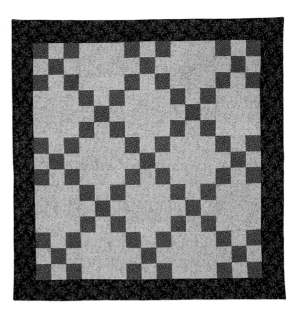

Nine-Patch A

Nine-Patch B

A Nine-Patch Color Placement Exercise

Nine Patch				
		A	**B**	
Size	Across Down	34" x 34" 5 blocks 5 blocks	34" x 34" 5 blocks 5 blocks	
Fabric (yd)	Dark Light	1 1	1 1	
Strips to Cut	Dark Light	8 - 2½" 5 - 2½"	9 - 2½" 4 - 2½"	
Blocks		13		
			13	
		12	12	

This exercise shows construction of two quilts (A and B) using a simple nine-patch primary block made up of alternated light and dark squares, with a light secondary blocks. Then, we add triangles in the corners of the secondary blocks to see the effect. The quilts are identical except that the color placement of the dark and light squares in the primary blocks is reversed. Note that the layout is the same with the alternated primary and secondary blocks. Note also that there is an uneven number of rows to ensure that the primary block appears in all corners.

These designs make very nice two color quilts. The blocks can be as small as 3" or as large as 12", if you cut the squares with the Easy Angle™.

The photographs show the two designs with the plain secondary block. To make either of these two quilts, cut the strips indicated in the table. The yardage requirements are for one or the other of the quilts, but not both. Dark fabric strips include strips for a single simple border. If you wish, you may substitute a different fabric border as in the photographs. If you do, you should probably get ½ yard of the different dark fabric. The following instructions show how to cut and make the pieces.

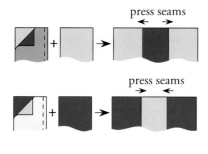

Sew the strips together. Press the seam toward the dark fabric. For the blocks with five light squares (quilt A), sew two sets of light-dark-light strips and one of dark-light-dark. For the blocks with five dark squares (quilt B), sew two sets of dark-light-dark and four sets of light-dark-light.

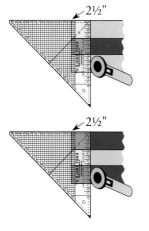

Now cross-cut the rows into 2½" bars using the Easy Angle II™. For quilt A, cut 26 light-dark-light bars and 13 dark-light-dark. For quilt B, cut 26 dark-light-dark bars and 13 light-dark-light bars.

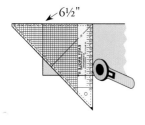

For the secondary blocks, cut twelve 6½" squares from the 6½" strips of light. Do this for either design.

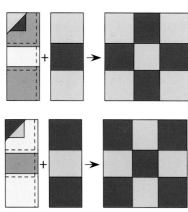

Sew the bars together to make the blocks for the design you want (quilt A or quilt B).

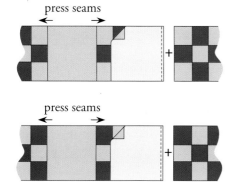

Sew the blocks together alternated with the plain secondary blocks. Sew three rows with three primary blocks and two rows with two primary blocks.

Sew the rows together from top to bottom. The layout is the same for both designs.

Cut four 2½" strips for the border. Sew border strips and bottom first and then to either side.

Now, by adding triangles in the corners of the same quilts, we will have an entirely different look.

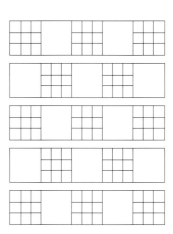

To add to the design of these simple nine-patch quilts, we will add triangles to the plain, light secondary blocks. Note that when we do this, we must cut pieces the proper size to ensure that the corners of these triangles meet the seams in the primary block when they are sewn together. In other words, the finished size of the triangle must be the same as the finished size of the small squares.

To get this, we will cut dark squares from strips the same width as we used for the primary block. Therefore we will use a 2½" strip. From one strip of dark fabric, cut 48 - 2½" squares.

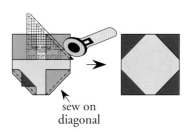

finished seams
must meet

Place one square right sides down in each corner of the secondary block. Place the ¼" line of the Easy Angle™ on the diagonal of the small square and trim along the edge of the tool to remove the corner of the small and large square. This gives you a perfect ¼" seam allowance when you sew.

Sew the corners on, turn the corners over and press.

With these secondary blocks, we get a whole new look to the original designs. Note that I removed some of the primary blocks in quilt B and replaced them with secondary blocks. Try your own design.

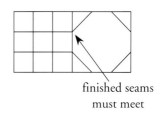

sew on
diagonal

Nine-Patch A with Triangles

Nine-Patch B with Triangles

Fox & Geese

In this quilt, we use the concept of alternating primary blocks and secondary blocks with triangles in the corners. We also introduce a Star Block as the primary block, and Flying Geese. You will see how the Easy Angle™ and Companion Angle™ work together to make cutting and construction of Flying Geese a real breeze.

The Star Block employs Flying Geese. In addition, we build a border using the Flying Geese units. The Flying Geese units in the Star Blocks are different than those in the border. The Star Block Flying Geese units use the light and dark fabrics. Since the star points need to stand out, the small triangles in each unit are dark and the large triangle is light. These light triangles, along with the light secondary block appear to form diamonds set on point.

The Flying Goose units in the border are made from the medium and light fabrics. The medium "geese" large triangles stand out from the light small triangles.

To get started, first measure and cut the number of strips of the light, medium, and dark fabrics indicated in the table.

Before making all of the blocks, make one Star Block to satisfy yourself of the color scheme you have chosen. Note especially if the star points stand out. If not, change fabrics before you make all of the blocks.

Fox and Geese		
Size	Across Down	45" x 45" 3 blocks 3 blocks with flying geese border
Fabric (yd)	Light Medium Dark	1¼ 1 1¼
Strips to Cut	Light Medium Dark	1 - 10½" 10 - 3" 1 - 5½" 7 - 3" 2 - 3" 9 - 1¾" 1 - 5½"
Blocks	(star block)	5
	(secondary block)	4
	(flying geese)	52

For the Star Block Flying Geese units, cut 20 Companion Angle™ triangles from the 3" strips of light fabric. For the border units, cut 52 Companion Angle™ triangles from the 3" strips of medium fabric.

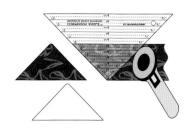

Then cut 40 Easy Angle™ triangles from the 3" strips of dark fabric. These can be cut with the fabrics right sides together. Similarly, cut 104 Easy Angle™ triangles from the light fabric.

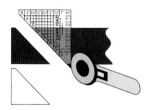

To make the Flying Geese units, sew two Easy Angle™ triangles to each Companion Angle™ triangle. Press seams toward the darker of the two fabrics. Trim the "dog-ears" at the lower two corners. Notice how the triangles fit perfectly together. Make 20 light and dark units for the Star Blocks and 104 medium and light units for the borders.

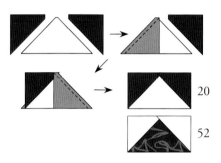

From the 3" medium strips, cut 16 - 3" squares for the corner triangles in the secondary blocks. From the 3" light strips, cut 20 - 3" squares for the corners of the Star Blocks.

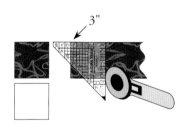

From the 5½" medium strip, cut 5 - 5½" squares for the centers of the Star Blocks.

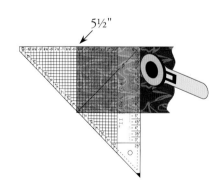

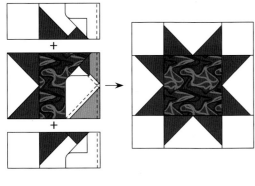

Lay out the 3" light squares, light and dark Flying Geese units, and the 5½" medium squares and sew them together. First sew a Flying Goose unit to two opposite sides of the medium square. Then sew a light square to either end of the Flying Goose units. Then sew these three rows together.

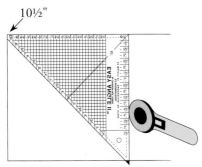

10½"

To make the secondary blocks, use the Easy Angle II™ to cut four 10½" squares from the 10½" strip of light fabric.

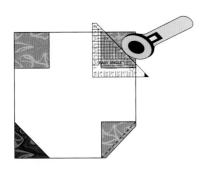

For each of the four blocks, place a 3" medium square right side down on each corner of the light 10½" square. Place the ¼" line of the Easy Angle™ on the diagonal of each small square and cut along the long edge of the tool to remove the corner. Sew along the diagonal and fold the triangle over the seam and press.

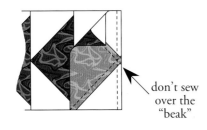

don't sew over the "beak"

Lay out the five Star Blocks and four secondary blocks in a 3 x 3 setting and sew them together in rows. Place the Star Blocks in the center and the four corners.

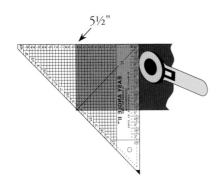

5½"

In order for the Flying Geese border to fit with this sized unit, the first border has to be finished at half the width of the Flying Geese units, or 1¼". The strips for the inner border must be cut 1¾". Add these simple borders first.

Next, sew four sets of 13 Flying Geese units. When you sew these together, watch closely so that you do not sew over the point or "beak" of the goose.

Sew one set to each of the two sides of the pieced top.

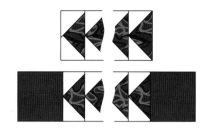

Then cut four 5½" squares of the dark fabric and sew one to each end of the remaining two sets of Flying Geese. Sew these two strips to the top and bottom.

Add a final border from the remaining 1¾" dark strips. You will have to cut one strip into four pieces and add it to each of four strips. When you attach the borders, begin sewing at the end where the short piece is attached.

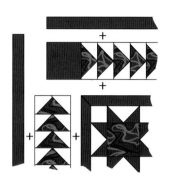

To complete the project, refer to *Finishing the Quilt*, which starts on page 6. Cut a backing fabric and batt to the proper size and layer the quilt, back right side down, batt in the center, and top right side up. Pin or baste, quilt as desired, bind and enjoy.

Determining Sizes and Yardage

Determining Sizes. How and where you plan to use the quilt will determine the color, the size, the weight of the batting, and how it is finished. To determine the size of a bed quilt, you should consider if is it to be used as a bedspread or a quilt for keeping warm. The first should be long enough to come to 2" from the floor or meet the dust ruffle. The second should come to the bottom of the mattress. You should also keep in mind the standard sizes of quilt batts as shown in the table.

BATTING SIZES	
TYPE	**SIZE (")**
Crib	45 x 60
Twin	72 x 90
Full	81 x 96
Queen	90 x 108
King	120 x 120

The weight of the batting depends on how you will finish the quilt. An extra-loft batt is fine for tying but impossible to hand quilt. A low-loft batt is very easy to quilt but has a flatter look. There are several steps you will take in determining your block size.

First consider a block consisting of squares and triangles. Now, using the Easy Angle™, you can cut squares and triangles from 1" strips all the way up to 4½" strips. Finished sizes of squares and triangles will range from ½" to 4". Consider these pieces in a nine-patch block. The finished block could be as small as 1½" or as large as 12". Be careful to consider the overall block size when considering the size of the pieces in the block. A 4" finished square may not seem too big, until it is part of a 12" nine-patch block.

Here is a simple sequence of steps you might take in determining size of a given finished quilt size:

- Determine the blocks (primary and secondary) you want to use. Also, determine if you want borders or sashing.

- Lay out the quilt design (e.g., on graph paper).

- Choose completed quilt size (e.g., king size).

- Determine unbordered quilt size (often the size of the mattress top).

- Determine finished block size based on quilt size (without borders) and the number of blocks. For example, a 72" x 90" finished quilt would require 80 - 9" square finished blocks in an 8 x 10 setting.

- Determine piece sizes in the block (e.g., a 9" square nine-patch requires 3" finished squares or triangles cut from 3½" strips).

Not all quilts need borders, but they do give a finished look to the edge. For the most part the borders on all the sides are equal in width. It is better to have two or three smaller borders totalling 10" (i.e., 2", 3", and 5") rather than a single 10" border. The exception is if you plan to quilt an elaborate design in the border. In that case, remember that quilting shows best on light, solid colors.

MATTRESS SIZES

TYPE	SIZE (")
Crib	28 x 52
Twin	39 x 75
Full	54 x 75
Queen	60 x 80
King	76 x 80

Figuring Yardage. This is a more involved process. The first thing is not to be afraid of buying too much fabric. It is far better to have some left over, than to run out. When figuring yardage, use a fabric width of 42". Let's figure yardage of a simple project. The example shown here uses six Shoo-Fly blocks with sashing. The blocks are nine-patch, with a finished width of 9". Therefore, the squares and triangles (as well as the sashing squares) have an unfinished size of 3½". The sashing strips are this wide and 9½" long. Now, let's figure the yardage:

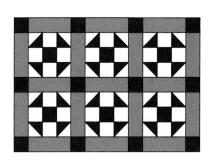

Sashing Fabric

> For 17 sashing strips 3½" by 9½", cut 9½" strips from the 42" wide fabric and cut 3½" strips from these as indicated.

> From each 9½" wide strip of fabric you will get 42" ÷ 3½" = 12 sashing strips. Therefore to get 17, you will cut two 9½" wide strips, requiring 2 x 9½" = 19" of fabric. To give myself some cushion, I would purchase ¾ yard.

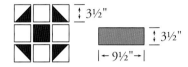

Light Fabric

> For every two 3" finished Easy Angle™ triangles, you will use approximately 4¼" from a 3½" wide strip. Since there are 4 (triangles per block) x 6 (blocks) = 24 triangles, you will use 4¼" x 12 = 51" for the triangles. You will need 51" ÷ 42" (fabric width) = 2 strips (rounded up).

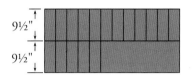

> From 3½" wide strips you will cut 4 (squares per block) x 6 (blocks) = 24 squares. The length of fabric is 3½" x 24 = 84". You will need 84" ÷ 42" (fabric width) = 2 strips (rounded up).

> Fabric needed is 4 (strips) x 3½" (strip width) = 14" of fabric. I would purchase at least ½ yard.

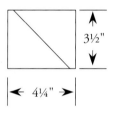

Dark Fabric

> You will need 2 strips for dark triangles (the same as for the light triangles).

> From 3½" wide strips you will cut 6 (1 per block) + 12 (sashing squares) = 18 squares. The length of fabric is 3½" x 18 = 63". You will need 63" ÷ 42" (fabric width) = 2 strips (rounded up).

> As for the light fabric, I would purchase ½ yard of the dark.

Caution: Directional fabric designs (e.g., hearts, animals, etc.) will sometimes turn sideways when strip pieced. If this bothers you, select fabric that has an overall pattern, without direction.

Color Planning Layouts

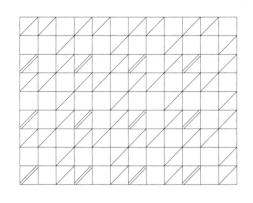

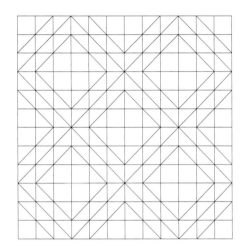

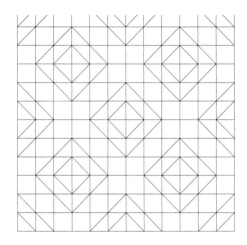

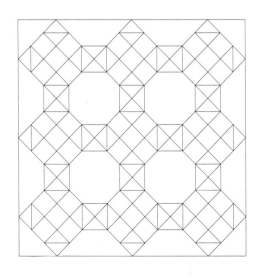

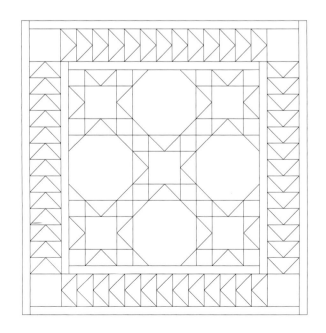

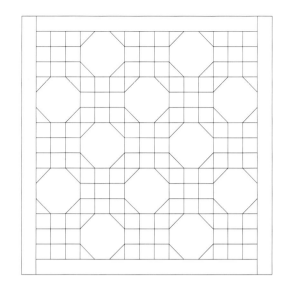
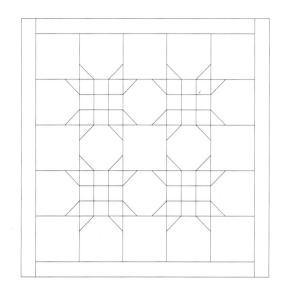
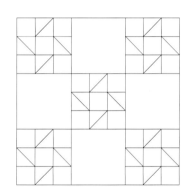
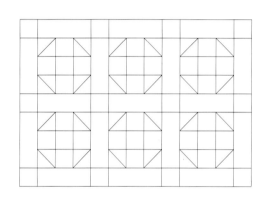
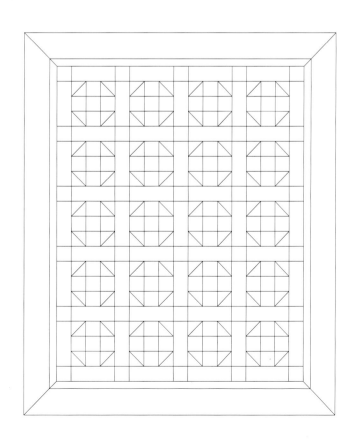

Books, Booklets, Tools and Videos
by Sharon Hultgren

Book and Video Series:

The Basics: Introduction to Quilting 101
Beyond the Basics: Quilting 201
Exploring New Shapes: Quilting 301
60° Shapes With No Math: Quilting 401

Other Books and Booklets:

Traditional Quilts the Easy Way
Traditional Quilts II the Easy Way
High Seas
Baby Blocks
Tumbling Stars
Double Diamonds
Bear of the North
My English Garden
Winter Pine
Stars Come Tumbling Down
Sapphire Star

Tools:

Easy Angle
Easy Angle II
Easy Hexagon
Easy Eight
Easy Six
Easy Three